A FIRST LOOK AT LEAVES

BY MILLICENT E. SELSAM
AND JOYCE HUNT

ILLUSTRATED BY HARRIETT SPRINGER

WALKER AND COMPANY
NEW YORK

For Ethan

The authors wish to thank DR.
HOWARD S. IRWIN, Executive Director
of the New York Botanical Garden,
for reading the text of this book.

Text copyright © 1972 by Millicent E. Selsam and Joyce Hunt

Published simultaneously in Canada by Fitzhenry & Whiteside, Limited, Toronto.

ISBN: 0-8027-6117-8
ISBN: 0-8027-6118-6

Library of Congress Catalog Card Number: 72-81376

First published in the United States of America in 1972 by the Walker Publishing Company, Inc.

Printed in the United States of America

A
FIRST LOOK AT
SERIES

Each of the nature books
for this series is planned to develop
the child's powers of observation
and give him or her a rudimentary grasp
of scientific classification.

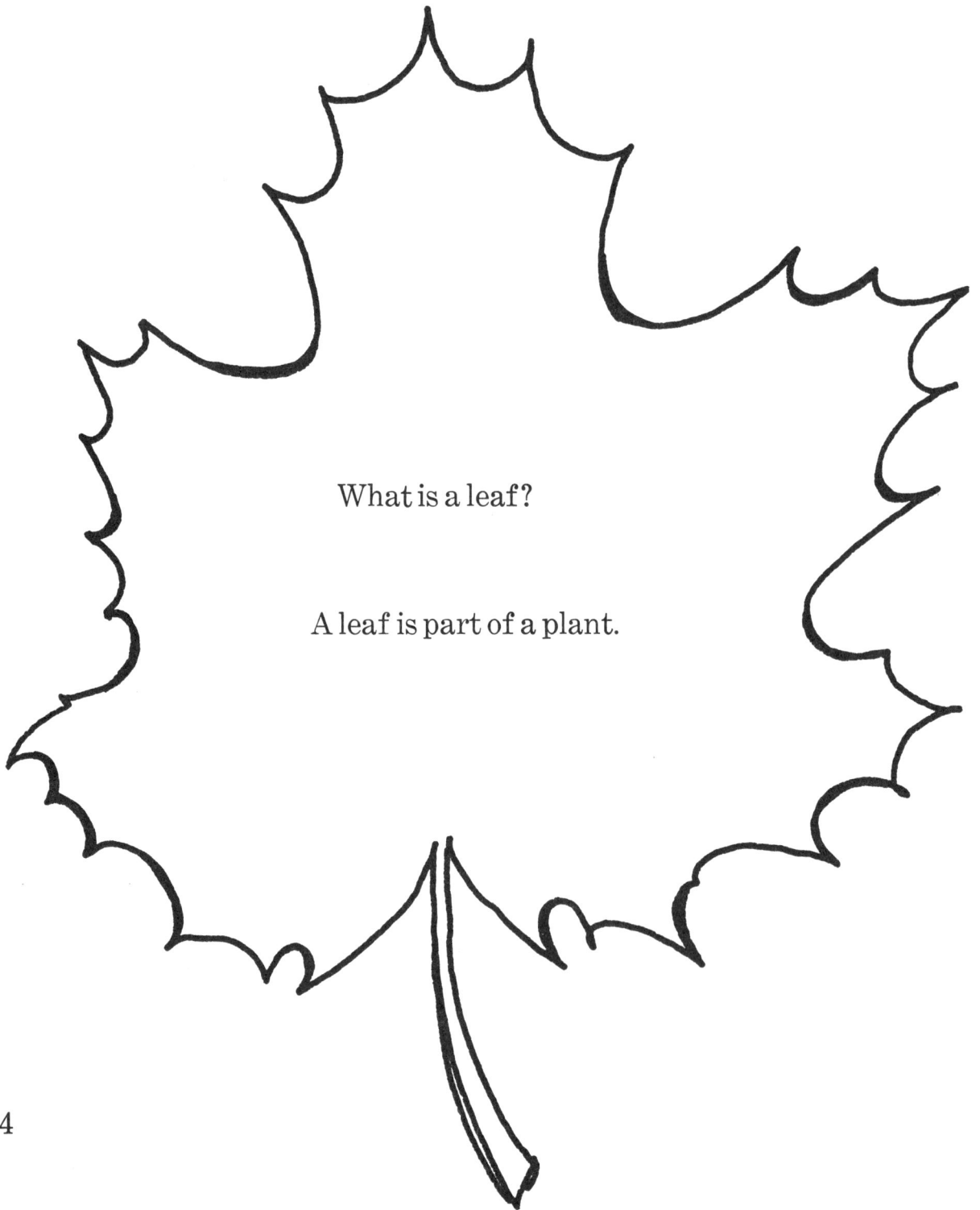

What is a leaf?

A leaf is part of a plant.

This is a plant with flowers and leaves.

Find the leaves.

A tree is also a plant.
It has leaves too.

Find the leaves.

Sometimes trees have leaves like needles.

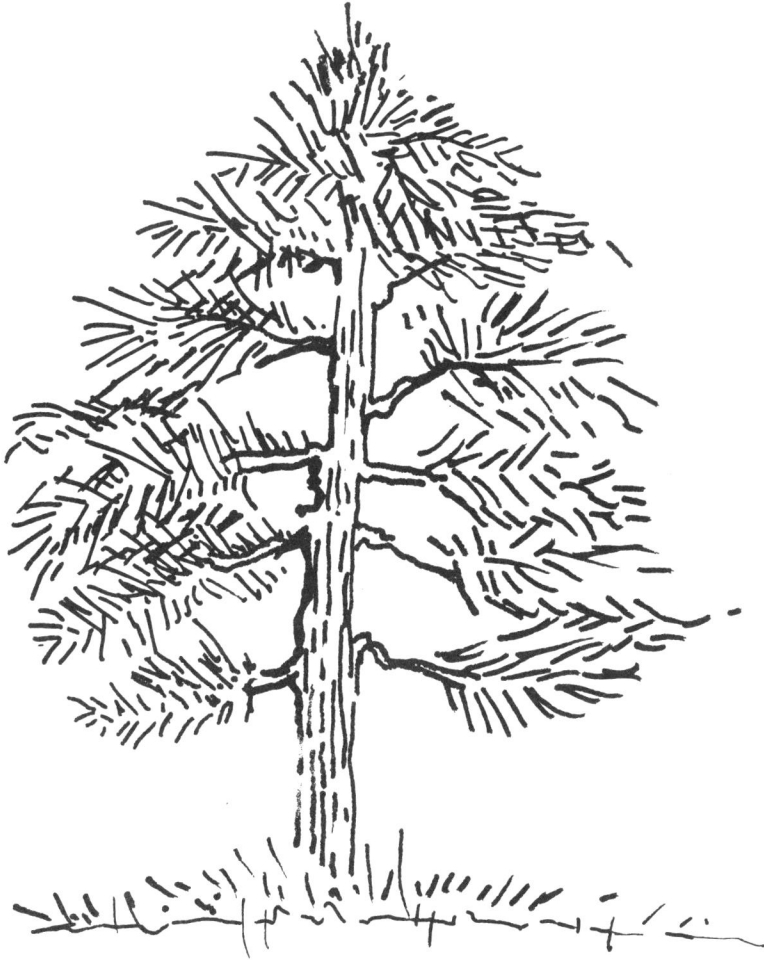

Find the leaves.

The leaves of grass are long and narrow.

Find the leaves.

Do the leaves of the plant
with flowers

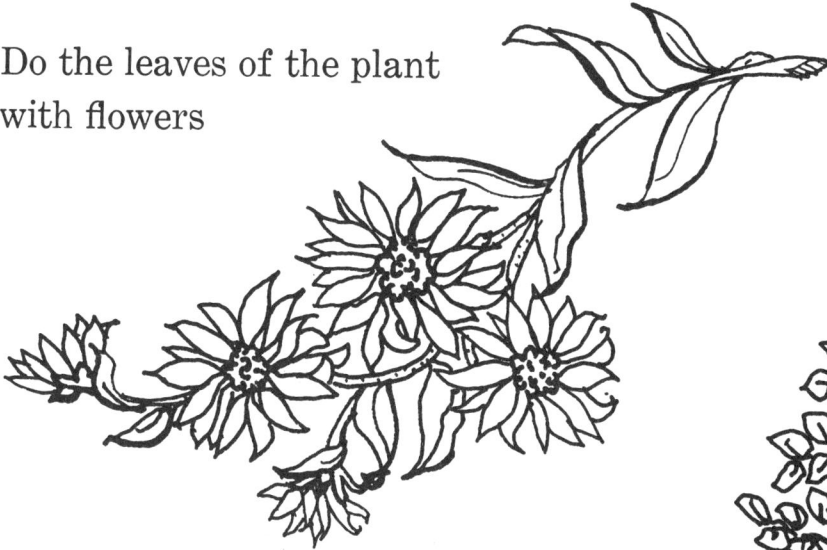

look the same
as the leaves in the tree

or the grass leaves?

No, they don't.
Leaves are different.

9

Find the round leaf.
Find the leaf that looks like a star.
Find the leaf that looks like a heart.

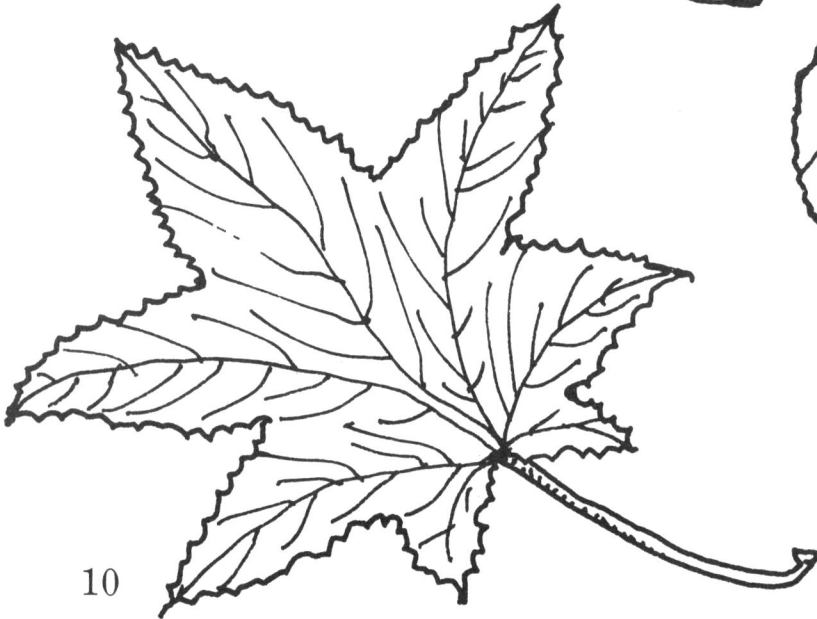

Find the leaf that looks like a needle.
Find the leaf that looks like a mitten.
Find the leaf that looks like a fan.

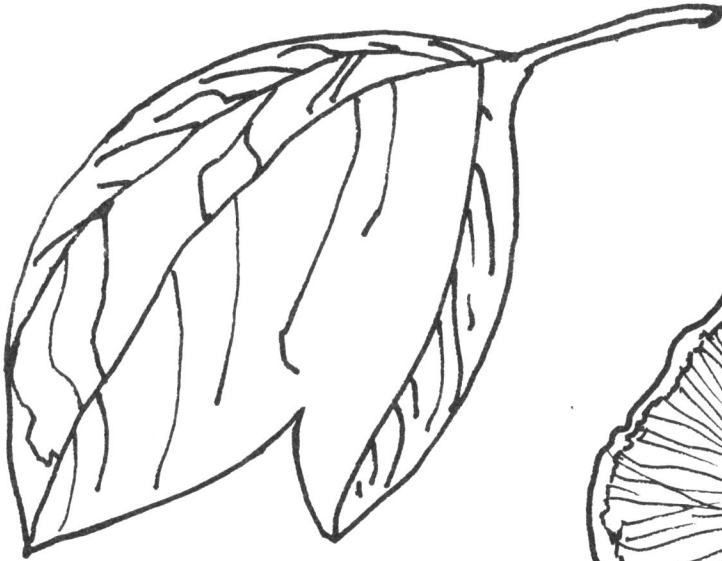

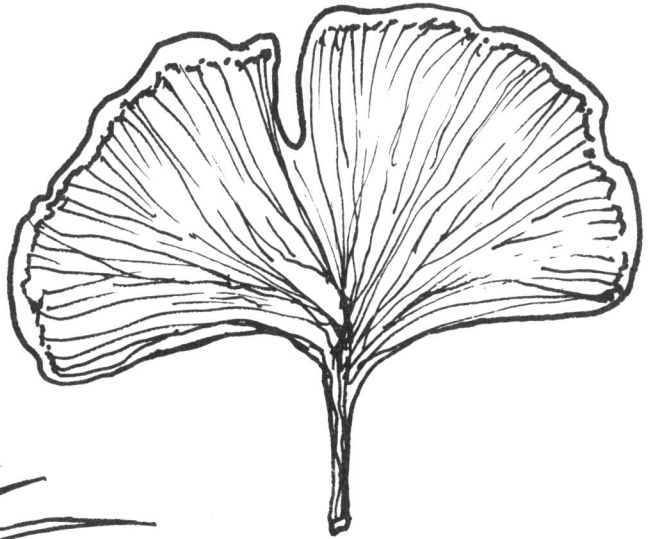

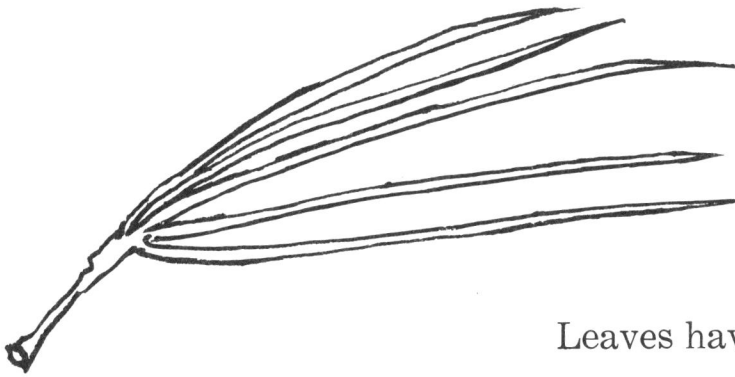

Leaves have different shapes.

There are other things to look for.

Find the leaf with a smooth edge.
Find the leaf with an edge like a saw.
Find the leaf with a wavy edge.

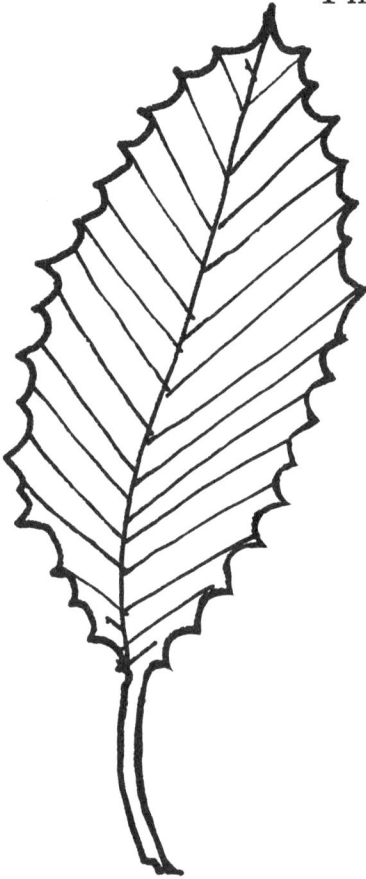

Leaves have different edges.

Some leaves look as though somebody took
a scissors and cut parts out of them.
The parts that remain are called lobes.
Find the leaf with pointed lobes.
Find the leaf with rounded lobes.

Sometimes a single leaf looks
like a lot of leaves.

But it is really all one leaf.

It is called a compound leaf.
Each part of the leaf is called a leaflet.

Sometimes there are a lot of leaves
on a stem and they *are* separate leaves.

Can you see anything new in this picture?

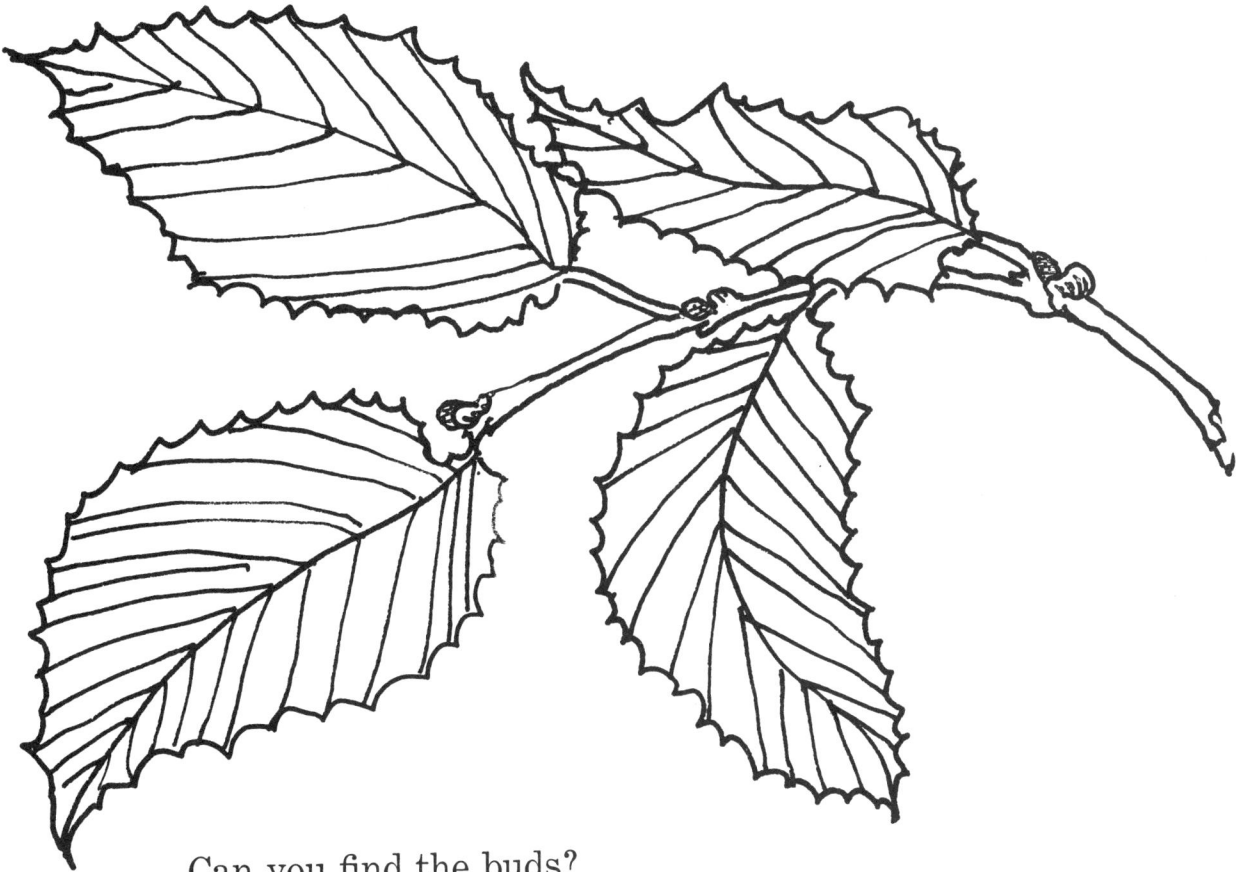

Can you find the buds?

A separate leaf with a bud at the bottom
is called a simple leaf.
If there is no bud at the bottom, it is a leaflet,
and is part of a compound leaf.

15

A puzzle:

16

Which are the simple leaves?

Which is the compound leaf?

Look to see where the buds are.

Another puzzle:

Is this a simple leaf or a compound leaf?

Even though the leaflets all come
together at one point, it is still
a compound leaf.

To prove it, look for the bud.

Still another puzzle!

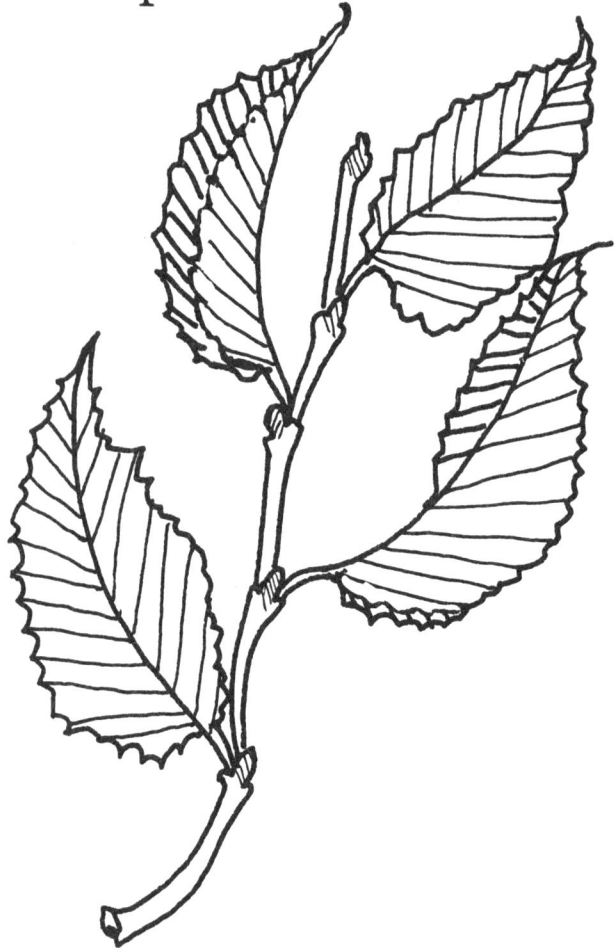

Can you tell the difference between these two pictures?
Some leaves come out of the stem opposite each other.
Some leaves do not come out of the stem
opposite each other.

Which is which?

Do any lines on these leaves look
like the veins in your hand?

These are leaf veins.
They carry water and minerals to the leaf.

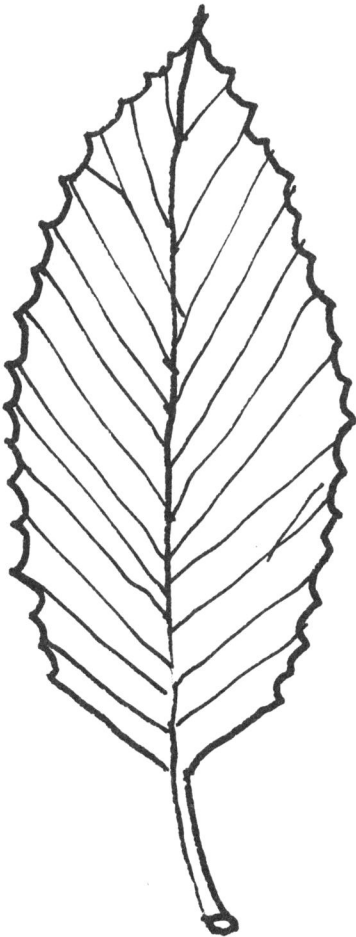

How do water and minerals get to a leaf
when it is high up on a tree?

First, the water and minerals
from the soil enter the roots.
Then they go through tiny tubes in the
trunk up to the veins in the leaves.
When the water and minerals get to the leaves,
they are used to make food for the whole plant.

Now you can find leaves that are round, or long,
or shaped like stars, fans, hearts, or needles.

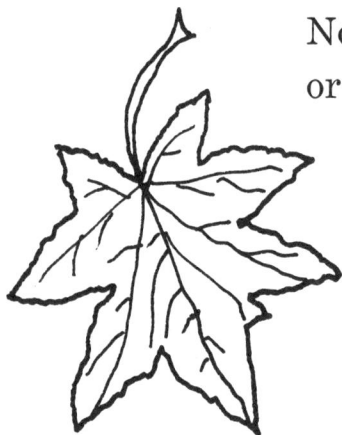

You can find leaves with smooth edges,
or wavy edges, or edges like saws.

You can find leaves that look as though
they were cut with a scissors.

You can find simple leaves and compound leaves
by looking for the bud.

You can find leaves that are opposite
on the stem or not opposite on the stem.

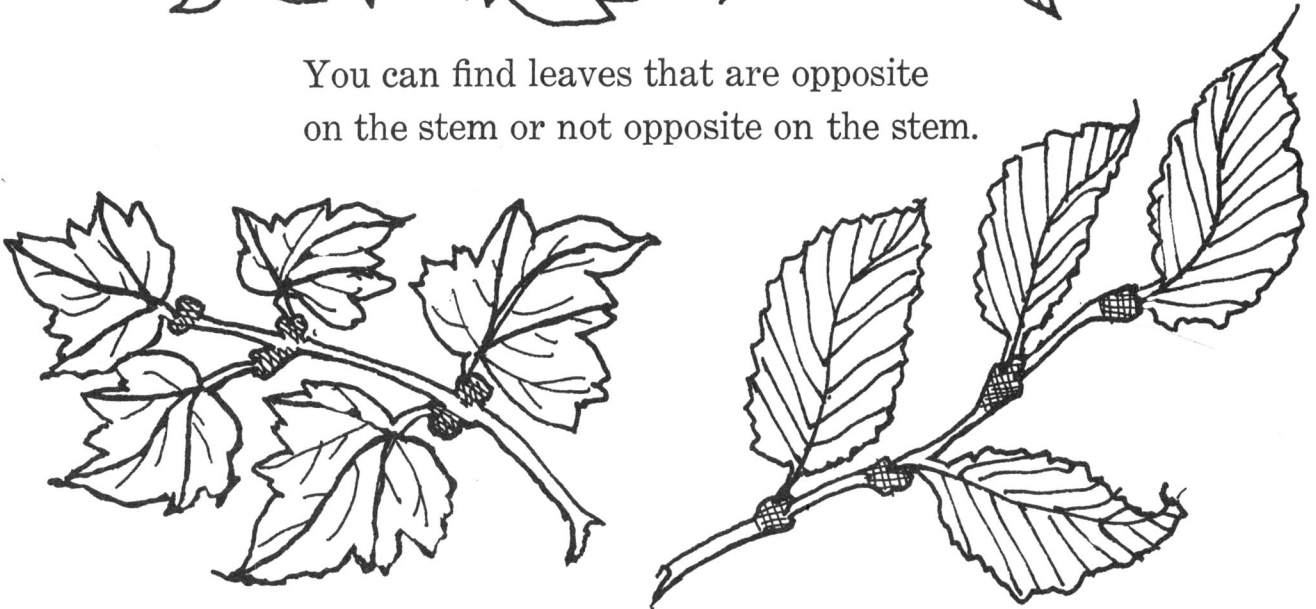

You can look for the veins in a leaf.

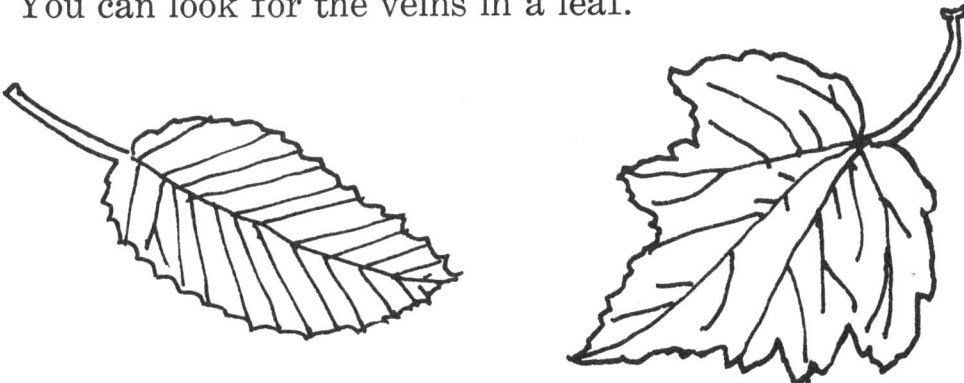

25

When you look at a leaf, you have to notice many things.
Here is a leaf of an oak tree.

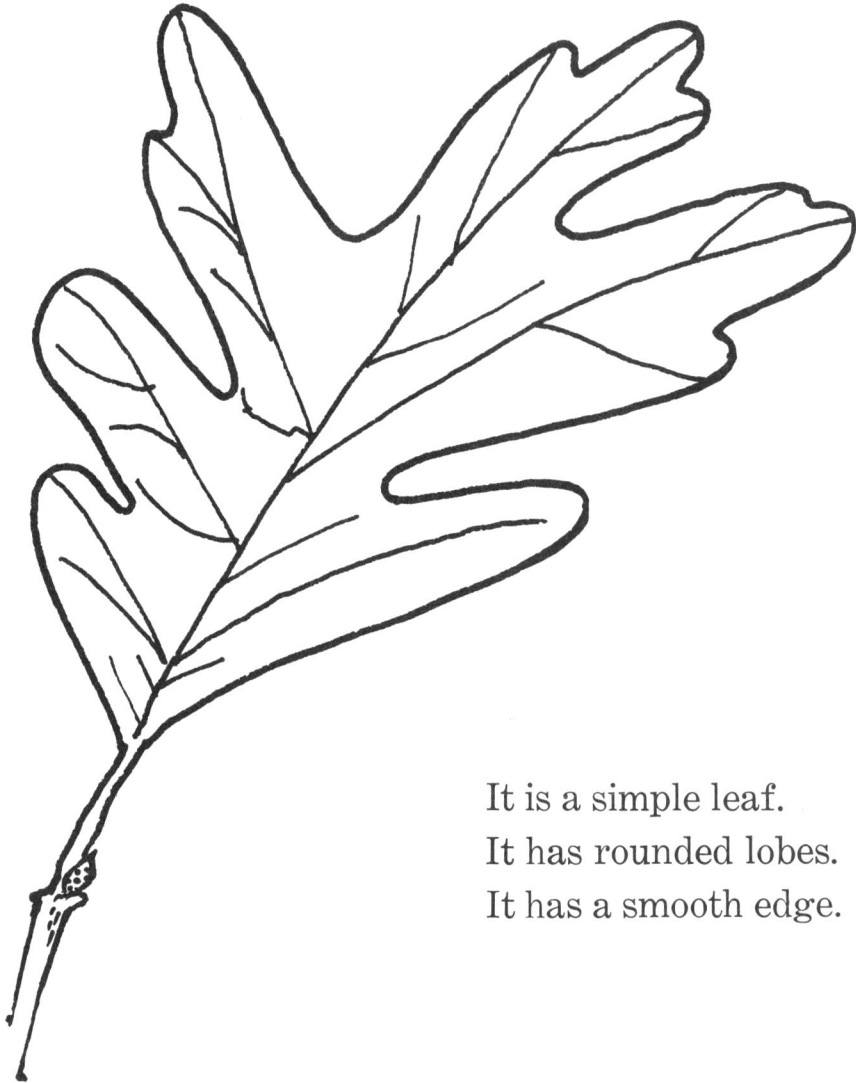

It is a simple leaf.
It has rounded lobes.
It has a smooth edge.

Here is a leaf of a walnut tree.

Can you describe it?

Is it simple or compound?

Does it have a smooth edge or an edge like a saw?

Here are the leaves of different trees.

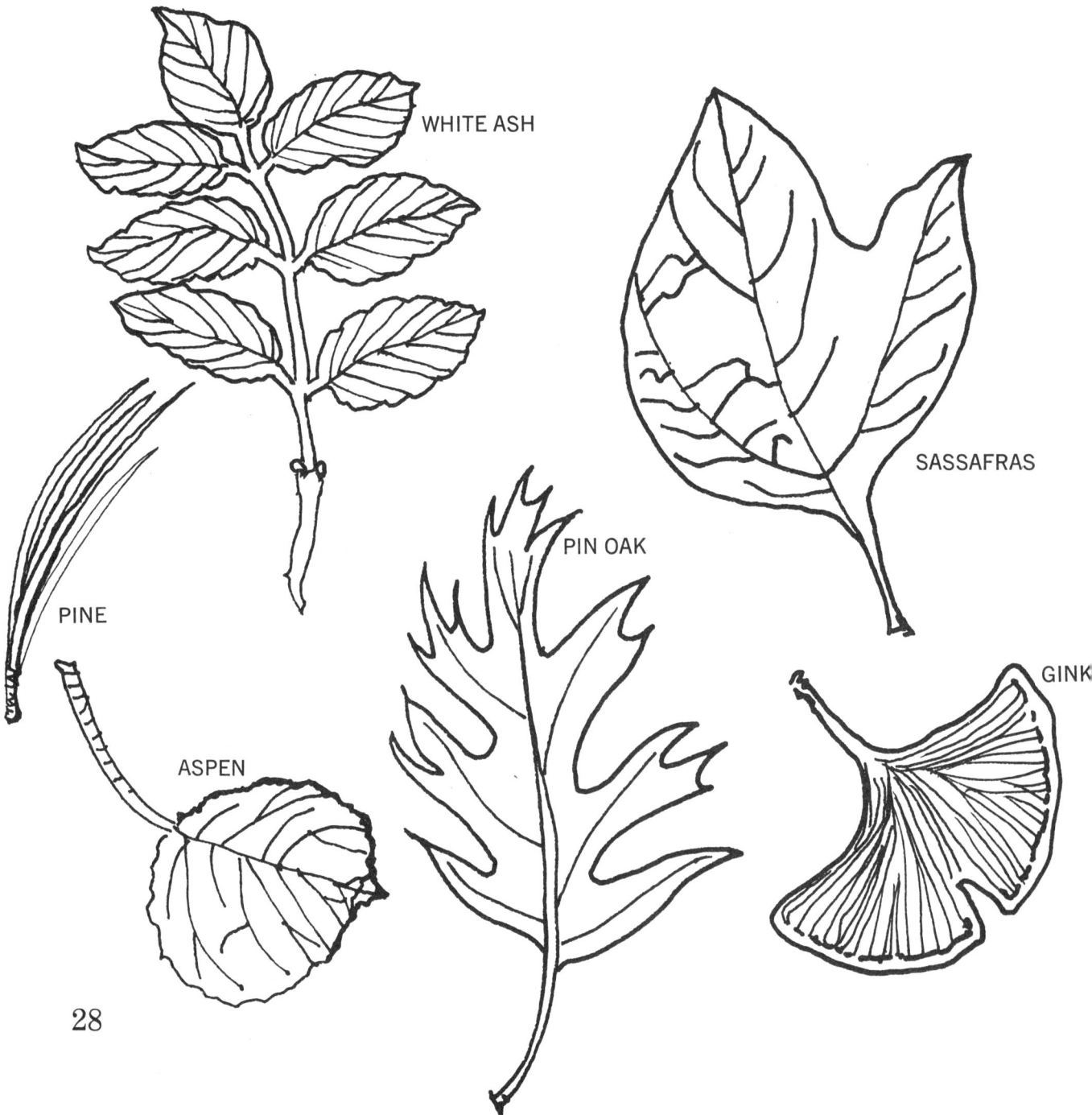

WHITE ASH

SASSAFRAS

PINE

PIN OAK

ASPEN

GINK

28

See if you can find leaves like these in
the park, on your street, or in the woods.

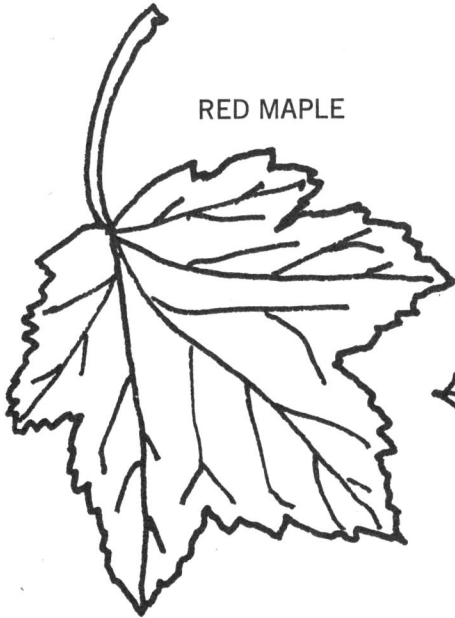

RED MAPLE

HORSE CHESTNUT

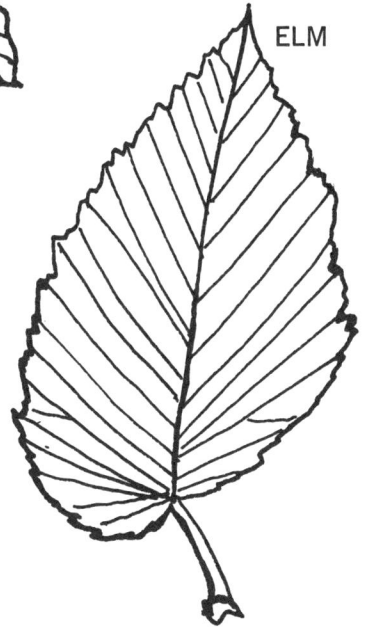

ELM

WHITE OAK

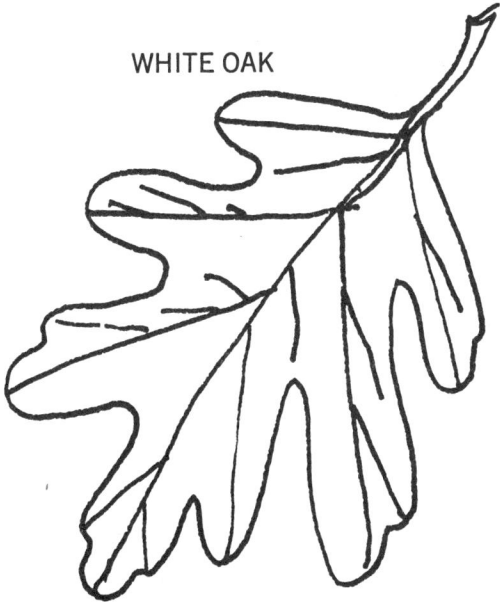

CATALPA

YOU CAN MAKE LEAF PRINTS

You will need:

an ink roller

printing ink

printing paper

a magazine with a smooth cover

tweezers

leaves

The ink roller, printing paper, and ink
can be bought in any art supply store.

1. Spread the newspaper on a table.

2. Put the magazine on the newspaper.

3. Squeeze out a blob of ink on the smooth surface of the magazine.

4. Spread the ink on the roller by rolling it back and forth.

5. Place the leaf on a clean piece of paper.

31

6. Spread the ink on the smooth side of the leaf.

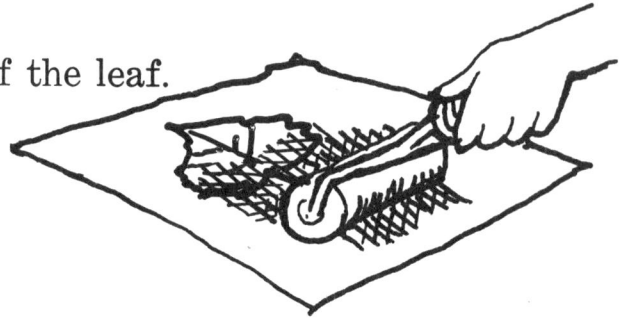

7. Lift the leaf with the tweezers and put it
   ink-face-down on the printing paper.

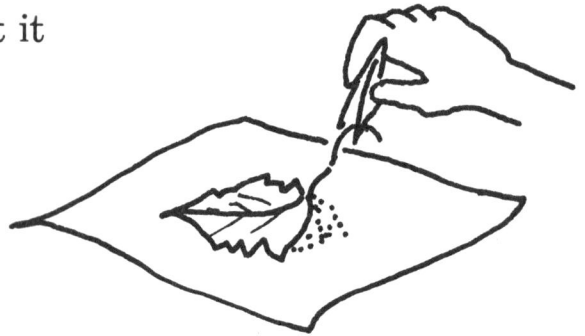

8. Put a clean piece of paper over the leaf
   and rub carefully with your hand.
   The leaf must not move.

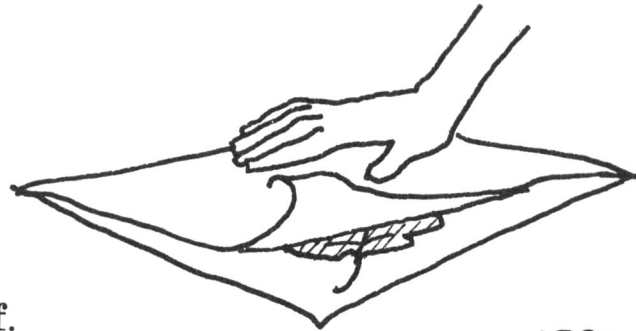

9. Remove the paper and pick up the leaf.
   Your leaf print is made.